SILENT OWLS

by Jenna Grodzicki

Minneapolis, Minnesota

Credits

Cover and title page, © charafeddine/iStock and © pchoui/iStock; 5, © blickwinkel/Alamy Stock Photo; 6BM, © davemhuntphotography/Shutterstock; 6BR, © Melani Wright/Adobe Stock Images; 6–7, © David Hoffmann/Adobe Stock Images; 9, © Vaclav Matous/Shutterstock; 10, © Berbegal Miguel Angel/Shutterstock; 11, © mauritius images GmbH/ Alamy Stock Photo; 12–13, © Rudmer Zwerver/Shutterstock; 14B, © Debra O'Connor/Shutterstock; 14–15, © scigelova/Shutterstock; 16, © Jay Ondreicka/Shutterstock; 17, © Bjorn Uitenbroek/Shutterstock; 18, © Maximillian cabinet/Shutterstock; 19, © Franz Christoph Robiller/ Alamy Stock Photo; 20–21, © Milan Zygmunt/Shutterstock; 22TR, © Sly/Adobe Stock Images; 22ML, © Carol Gray/Adobe Stock Images; 22BR, © Mauricio/Adobe Stock Images; 23, © WildlifeWorld/Shutterstock

Bearport Publishing Company Product Development Team

Publisher: Jen Jenson; Director of Product Development: Spencer Brinker; Editorial Director: Allison Juda; Editor: Cole Nelson; Editor: Tiana Tran; Production Editor: Naomi Reich; Art Director: Kim Jones; Designer: Kayla Eggert; Designer: Steve Scheluchin; Production Specialist: Owen Hamlin

Statement on Usage of Generative Artificial Intelligence

Bearport Publishing remains committed to publishing high-quality nonfiction books. Therefore, we restrict the use of generative AI to ensure accuracy of all text and visual components pertaining to a book's subject. See BearportPublishing.com for details.

Library of Congress Cataloging-in-Publication Data is available at www.loc.gov or upon request from the publisher.

ISBN: 979-8-89577-058-0 (hardcover)
ISBN: 979-8-89577-175-4 (ebook)

Copyright © 2026 Bearport Publishing Company. All rights reserved. No part of this publication may be reproduced in whole or in part, stored in any retrieval system, or transmitted in any form or by any means, electronic, mechanical, photocopying, recording, or otherwise, without written permission from the publisher. Bearport Publishing is a division of FlutterBee Education Group.

For more information, write to Bearport Publishing, 3500 American Blvd W, Suite 150, Bloomington, MN 55431.

CONTENTS

Terror in the Night Sky 4

Deadly Raptors. 6

Nowhere to Hide 8

Night Birds 10

Hunting with Style 12

Silent Strike 14

Swallowed Whole. 16

Fierce Families 18

Learning to Hunt 20

Meet the Birds 22
Glossary 23
Index 24
Read More 24
Learn More Online 24
About the Author. 24

TERROR IN THE NIGHT SKY

Darkness has fallen, and an owl is on the hunt. The silent bird flies through the night, searching for its dinner. As it soars over the forest floor, it spots a mouse scurrying by. The owl swoops down and snatches up the little critter. Then, this fearsome **raptor** feasts on its meal.

Throughout history, people around the world have thought of owls as symbols of wisdom.

Some owls can carry up to 5 pounds (2.3 kg) while flying.

DEADLY RAPTORS

Raptors are some of the most skilled hunters in the animal kingdom. Also known as birds of **prey**, these fearsome creatures are often **apex predators** in their **habitats**, attacking other creatures while rarely being hunted themselves. Incredible eyesight, sensitive hearing, supersharp talons, and hooked beaks make raptors especially skilled hunters.

Beak

Talon

The word *raptor* comes from a word meaning to take away by force.

Red-tailed hawks are also raptors.

NOWHERE TO HIDE

There are very few places on Earth where prey is safe from owls. More than 200 owl **species** fly the skies of every continent except Antarctica. They stalk their prey in forests, grasslands, tundra, and deserts. Because owls can turn their heads almost all the way around, these raptors can see everything that moves nearby.

Many owls use **camouflage** to blend in with their habitat. This allows them to easily hunt without being seen.

9

NIGHT BIRDS

Most owls are **nocturnal**, meaning they are awake and active at night. These nighttime hunters eat small rodents, fish, insects, rabbits, snakes, lizards, and even other birds. Owls have excellent night vision and sensitive hearing—senses that help them hunt in the dark.

Not all owls are nocturnal. Some hunt during the day, while others hunt at dusk or dawn.

Owls have big eyes that catch a lot of light and help them see well at night.

HUNTING WITH STYLE

Like other raptors, owls strike their prey from above. Some owls search for food while **perched** on a tree branch or tall building. Others glide on the wind, carefully watching below. When owls spot something tasty, the deadly hunters dive to attack. They are almost completely silent as they fly, allowing them to surprise their unlucky prey.

A few owls, such as burrowing owls, run after their prey on the ground.

SILENT STRIKE

How do owls fly so silently? The birds have feathers that muffle almost all sound from their velvety soft wings. Also, their wings are bigger in relation to their bodies when compared to most other birds. This allows them to fly very slowly without flapping as much.

Sometimes, owls eat their prey right away. But other times, they carry it home to eat.

SWALLOWED WHOLE

After catching prey, owls don't chew. The birds swallow smaller animals whole and use their sharp beaks to tear larger prey into smaller chunks. They quickly swallow their meals, however, owls can't **digest** all parts of their food. About 10 hours after eating, they cough up oval-shaped pellets containing undigested feathers, fur, teeth, and bones.

Owls usually cough up one pellet each day.

Some owls hide their food to save for later. This is called caching (KASH-ing).

FIERCE FAMILIES

Most owls live alone, except when it's time to **mate**. Once two owls mate, they live together in a nest, tree hole, or even a shallow indentation on the ground. The **female** lays up to 14 eggs in this home. About a month later, these eggs hatch into babies called owlets.

Most owl eggs are all white, but some have specks of brown.

After their eggs hatch, the **male** parent hunts for food, which the female tears apart to feed to her owlets.

LEARNING TO HUNT

Owlets grow quickly. They learn to fly and hunt by watching their parents. It takes only a couple of months before they can take off from the nest themselves. A few months after that, they fly away for good as fully grown birds of prey, ready to take to the skies and hunt on their own.

Great horned owls can live for more than 20 years in the wild.

MEET THE BIRDS

There are more than 200 species of owls. Let's take a look at a few of them.

Great Horned Owl
Great horned owls are often called the Tigers of the Sky. This is because they can take down prey that is larger and heavier than they are. Sometimes, they even hunt other birds of prey!

Snowy Owl
Snowy owls share their Arctic tundra homes with lemmings—their favorite meal. Lemmings often hide under several inches of snow, but that doesn't stop snowy owls from finding them. The birds use their excellent hearing to listen for their buried prey.

Burrowing Owl
Burrowing owls are some of the smallest kinds of owl. They live in underground holes in Central America, South America, and the western United States. While burrowing owls can fly, they usually hunt on foot.

GLOSSARY

apex predators animals that hunt without being hunted by any other animals

camouflage coloring that makes animals look like their surroundings

digest to break down food inside the body

female an owl that can lay eggs

habitats the natural environments of plants and animals

male an owl that cannot lay eggs

mate to come together to have young

nocturnal active at night

perched sitting or standing on a high place

prey animals that are eaten by other animals

raptor large, strong birds with hooked beaks and large talons that eat mostly meat

species groups of living things that are similar and can have young together

INDEX

apex predators 6
beak 6, 8, 16
eggs 18–19
feathers 14, 16
hunting 4, 6, 9–10, 12, 19–20
mating 18
nocturnal 10
owlets 18–20
pellets 16
prey 6, 8, 12, 15–16, 20, 22
raptor 4, 6–8, 12
talons 6, 8

READ MORE

Davis-Castro, Janet. *Owls (Birds of Prey).* Mankato, MN: Black Rabbit Books, 2023.

Markle, Sandra. *On the Hunt with Owls (Ultimate Predators).* Minneapolis: Lerner Publications, 2023.

LEARN MORE ONLINE

1. Go to **FactSurfer.com** or scan the QR code below.
2. Enter "**Silent Owls**" into the search box.
3. Click on the cover of this book to see a list of websites.

ABOUT THE AUTHOR

Jenna Grodzicki is the author of more than 30 books for children. She lives on beautiful Cape Cod with her husband and two children, where she is both a library media specialist and a writer.